Lineup Card

Team	Opponent
Coach	Coach

Order	No.	Starter	Pos.	No.	Substitute
1					
2					
3					
4					
5					
6					
7					
8					
9					
10					
11					
12					
13					
14					
15					
16					
17					
18					
19					

Notes

Home:	Date:	Umpire:
Away:	Location:	Scorer:

#	Player	P	1	2	3	4	5	6	7	8	9	10	AB	H	BB	RBI	R
Runs																	

Lineup Card

Team	Opponent
Coach	Coach

Order	No.	Starter	Pos.	No.	Substitute
1					
2					
3					
4					
5					
6					
7					
8					
9					
10					
11					
12					
13					
14					
15					
16					
17					
18					
19					

Notes

Home:	Date:	Umpire:
Away:	Location:	Scorer:

#	Player	P	1	2	3	4	5	6	7	8	9	10	AB	H	BB	RBI	R
Runs																	

Lineup Card

Team	Opponent
Coach	Coach

Order	No.	Starter	Pos.	No.	Substitute
1					
2					
3					
4					
5					
6					
7					
8					
9					
10					
11					
12					
13					
14					
15					
16					
17					
18					
19					

Notes

Home:	Date:	Umpire:
Away:	Location:	Scorer:

#	Player	P	1	2	3	4	5	6	7	8	9	10	AB	H	BB	RBI	R
Runs																	

Lineup Card

Team	Opponent
Coach	Coach

Order	No.	Starter	Pos.	No.	Substitute
1					
2					
3					
4					
5					
6					
7					
8					
9					
10					
11					
12					
13					
14					
15					
16					
17					
18					
19					

Notes

Home:	Date:	Umpire:
Away:	Location:	Scorer:

#	Player	P	1	2	3	4	5	6	7	8	9	10	AB	H	BB	RBI	R
Runs																	

Lineup Card

Team	Opponent
Coach	Coach

Order	No.	Starter	Pos.	No.	Substitute
1					
2					
3					
4					
5					
6					
7					
8					
9					
10					
11					
12					
13					
14					
15					
16					
17					
18					
19					

Notes

Home:	Date:	Umpire:
Away:	Location:	Scorer:

#	Player	P	1	2	3	4	5	6	7	8	9	10	AB	H	BB	RBI	R
Runs																	

Lineup Card

Team	Opponent
Coach	Coach

Order	No.	Starter	Pos.	No.	Substitute
1					
2					
3					
4					
5					
6					
7					
8					
9					
10					
11					
12					
13					
14					
15					
16					
17					
18					
19					

Notes

Home:	Date:	Umpire:
Away:	Location:	Scorer:

#	Player	P	1	2	3	4	5	6	7	8	9	10	AB	H	BB	RBI	R
Runs																	

Lineup Card

Team	Opponent
Coach	Coach

Order	No.	Starter	Pos.	No.	Substitute
1					
2					
3					
4					
5					
6					
7					
8					
9					
10					
11					
12					
13					
14					
15					
16					
17					
18					
19					

Notes

Home:	Date:	Umpire:
Away:	Location:	Scorer:

#	Player	P	1	2	3	4	5	6	7	8	9	10	AB	H	BB	RBI	R
Runs																	

Lineup Card

Team	Opponent
Coach	Coach

Order	No.	Starter	Pos.	No.	Substitute
1					
2					
3					
4					
5					
6					
7					
8					
9					
10					
11					
12					
13					
14					
15					
16					
17					
18					
19					

Notes

Home:	Date:	Umpire:
Away:	Location:	Scorer:

#	Player	P	1	2	3	4	5	6	7	8	9	10	AB	H	BB	RBI	R
Runs																	

Lineup Card

Team	Opponent
Coach	Coach

Order	No.	Starter	Pos.	No.	Substitute
1					
2					
3					
4					
5					
6					
7					
8					
9					
10					
11					
12					
13					
14					
15					
16					
17					
18					
19					

Notes

Home:	Date:	Umpire:
Away:	Location:	Scorer:

#	Player	P	1	2	3	4	5	6	7	8	9	10	AB	H	BB	RBI	R
Runs																	

Lineup Card

Team	Opponent
Coach	Coach

Order	No.	Starter	Pos.	No.	Substitute
1					
2					
3					
4					
5					
6					
7					
8					
9					
10					
11					
12					
13					
14					
15					
16					
17					
18					
19					

Notes

Home:	Date:	Umpire:
Away:	Location:	Scorer:

#	Player	P	1	2	3	4	5	6	7	8	9	10	AB	H	BB	RBI	R
Runs																	

Lineup Card

Team	Opponent
Coach	Coach

Order	No.	Starter	Pos.	No.	Substitute
1					
2					
3					
4					
5					
6					
7					
8					
9					
10					
11					
12					
13					
14					
15					
16					
17					
18					
19					

Notes

Home:	Date:	Umpire:
Away:	Location:	Scorer:

#	Player	P	1	2	3	4	5	6	7	8	9	10	AB	H	BB	RBI	R
Runs																	

Lineup Card

Team	Opponent
Coach	Coach

Order	No.	Starter	Pos.	No.	Substitute
1					
2					
3					
4					
5					
6					
7					
8					
9					
10					
11					
12					
13					
14					
15					
16					
17					
18					
19					

Notes

Home:	Date:	Umpire:
Away:	Location:	Scorer:

#	Player	P	1	2	3	4	5	6	7	8	9	10	AB	H	BB	RBI	R
Runs																	

Lineup Card

Team	Opponent
Coach	Coach

Order	No.	Starter	Pos.	No.	Substitute
1					
2					
3					
4					
5					
6					
7					
8					
9					
10					
11					
12					
13					
14					
15					
16					
17					
18					
19					

Notes

Home:	Date:	Umpire:
Away:	Location:	Scorer:

#	Player	P	1	2	3	4	5	6	7	8	9	10	AB	H	BB	RBI	R
Runs																	

Lineup Card

Team	Opponent
Coach	Coach

Order	No.	Starter	Pos.	No.	Substitute
1					
2					
3					
4					
5					
6					
7					
8					
9					
10					
11					
12					
13					
14					
15					
16					
17					
18					
19					

Notes

Home:	Date:	Umpire:
Away:	Location:	Scorer:

#	Player	P	1	2	3	4	5	6	7	8	9	10	AB	H	BB	RBI	R
Runs																	

Lineup Card

Team	Opponent
Coach	Coach

Order	No.	Starter	Pos.	No.	Substitute
1					
2					
3					
4					
5					
6					
7					
8					
9					
10					
11					
12					
13					
14					
15					
16					
17					
18					
19					

Notes

Home:	Date:	Umpire:
Away:	Location:	Scorer:

#	Player	P	1	2	3	4	5	6	7	8	9	10	AB	H	BB	RBI	R
Runs																	

Lineup Card

Team	Opponent
Coach	Coach

Order	No.	Starter	Pos.	No.	Substitute
1					
2					
3					
4					
5					
6					
7					
8					
9					
10					
11					
12					
13					
14					
15					
16					
17					
18					
19					

Notes

Home:	Date:	Umpire:
Away:	Location:	Scorer:

#	Player	P	1	2	3	4	5	6	7	8	9	10	AB	H	BB	RBI	R
Runs																	

Lineup Card

Team	Opponent
Coach	Coach

Order	No.	Starter	Pos.	No.	Substitute
1					
2					
3					
4					
5					
6					
7					
8					
9					
10					
11					
12					
13					
14					
15					
16					
17					
18					
19					

Notes

Home:	Date:	Umpire:
Away:	Location:	Scorer:

#	Player	P	1	2	3	4	5	6	7	8	9	10	AB	H	BB	RBI	R
Runs																	

Lineup Card

Team	Opponent
Coach	Coach

Order	No.	Starter	Pos.	No.	Substitute
1					
2					
3					
4					
5					
6					
7					
8					
9					
10					
11					
12					
13					
14					
15					
16					
17					
18					
19					

Notes

Home:	Date:	Umpire:
Away:	Location:	Scorer:

#	Player	P	1	2	3	4	5	6	7	8	9	10	AB	H	BB	RBI	R
Runs																	

Lineup Card

Team	Opponent
Coach	**Coach**

Order	No.	Starter	Pos.	No.	Substitute
1					
2					
3					
4					
5					
6					
7					
8					
9					
10					
11					
12					
13					
14					
15					
16					
17					
18					
19					

Notes

Home:	Date:	Umpire:
Away:	Location:	Scorer:

#	Player	P	1	2	3	4	5	6	7	8	9	10	AB	H	BB	RBI	R
Runs																	

Lineup Card

Team	Opponent
Coach	Coach

Order	No.	Starter	Pos.	No.	Substitute
1					
2					
3					
4					
5					
6					
7					
8					
9					
10					
11					
12					
13					
14					
15					
16					
17					
18					
19					

Notes

Home:	Date:	Umpire:
Away:	Location:	Scorer:

#	Player	P	1	2	3	4	5	6	7	8	9	10	AB	H	BB	RBI	R
Runs																	

Lineup Card

Team	Opponent
Coach	Coach

Order	No.	Starter	Pos.	No.	Substitute
1					
2					
3					
4					
5					
6					
7					
8					
9					
10					
11					
12					
13					
14					
15					
16					
17					
18					
19					

Notes

Home:	Date:	Umpire:
Away:	Location:	Scorer:

#	Player	P	1	2	3	4	5	6	7	8	9	10	AB	H	BB	RBI	R
Runs																	

Lineup Card

Team	Opponent
Coach	Coach

Order	No.	Starter	Pos.	No.	Substitute
1					
2					
3					
4					
5					
6					
7					
8					
9					
10					
11					
12					
13					
14					
15					
16					
17					
18					
19					

Notes

Home:	Date:	Umpire:
Away:	Location:	Scorer:

#	Player	P	1	2	3	4	5	6	7	8	9	10	AB	H	BB	RBI	R
Runs																	

Lineup Card

Team	Opponent
Coach	Coach

Order	No.	Starter	Pos.	No.	Substitute
1					
2					
3					
4					
5					
6					
7					
8					
9					
10					
11					
12					
13					
14					
15					
16					
17					
18					
19					

Notes

Home:	Date:	Umpire:
Away:	Location:	Scorer:

#	Player	P	1	2	3	4	5	6	7	8	9	10	AB	H	BB	RBI	R
Runs																	

Lineup Card

Team	Opponent
Coach	Coach

Order	No.	Starter	Pos.	No.	Substitute
1					
2					
3					
4					
5					
6					
7					
8					
9					
10					
11					
12					
13					
14					
15					
16					
17					
18					
19					

Notes

Home:	Date:	Umpire:
Away:	Location:	Scorer:

#	Player	P	1	2	3	4	5	6	7	8	9	10	AB	H	BB	RBI	R
Runs																	

Lineup Card

Team	Opponent
Coach	Coach

Order	No.	Starter	Pos.	No.	Substitute
1					
2					
3					
4					
5					
6					
7					
8					
9					
10					
11					
12					
13					
14					
15					
16					
17					
18					
19					

Notes

Home:	Date:	Umpire:
Away:	Location:	Scorer:

#	Player	P	1	2	3	4	5	6	7	8	9	10	AB	H	BB	RBI	R
Runs																	

Lineup Card

Team	Opponent
Coach	Coach

Order	No.	Starter	Pos.	No.	Substitute
1					
2					
3					
4					
5					
6					
7					
8					
9					
10					
11					
12					
13					
14					
15					
16					
17					
18					
19					

Notes

Home:	Date:	Umpire:
Away:	Location:	Scorer:

#	Player	P	1	2	3	4	5	6	7	8	9	10	AB	H	BB	RBI	R
Runs																	

Lineup Card

Team	Opponent
Coach	Coach

Order	No.	Starter	Pos.	No.	Substitute
1					
2					
3					
4					
5					
6					
7					
8					
9					
10					
11					
12					
13					
14					
15					
16					
17					
18					
19					

Notes

Home:	Date:	Umpire:
Away:	Location:	Scorer:

#	Player	P	1	2	3	4	5	6	7	8	9	10	AB	H	BB	RBI	R
Runs																	

Lineup Card

Team	Opponent
Coach	Coach

Order	No.	Starter	Pos.	No.	Substitute
1					
2					
3					
4					
5					
6					
7					
8					
9					
10					
11					
12					
13					
14					
15					
16					
17					
18					
19					

Notes

Home:	Date:	Umpire:
Away:	Location:	Scorer:

#	Player	P	1	2	3	4	5	6	7	8	9	10	AB	H	BB	RBI	R
Runs																	

Lineup Card

Team	Opponent
Coach	Coach

Order	No.	Starter	Pos.	No.	Substitute
1					
2					
3					
4					
5					
6					
7					
8					
9					
10					
11					
12					
13					
14					
15					
16					
17					
18					
19					

Notes

Home:	Date:	Umpire:
Away:	Location:	Scorer:

#	Player	P	1	2	3	4	5	6	7	8	9	10	AB	H	BB	RBI	R
Runs																	

Lineup Card

Team	Opponent
Coach	Coach

Order	No.	Starter	Pos.	No.	Substitute
1					
2					
3					
4					
5					
6					
7					
8					
9					
10					
11					
12					
13					
14					
15					
16					
17					
18					
19					

Notes

Home:	Date:	Umpire:
Away:	Location:	Scorer:

#	Player	P	1	2	3	4	5	6	7	8	9	10	AB	H	BB	RBI	R
Runs																	

Lineup Card

Team	Opponent
Coach	Coach

Order	No.	Starter	Pos.	No.	Substitute
1					
2					
3					
4					
5					
6					
7					
8					
9					
10					
11					
12					
13					
14					
15					
16					
17					
18					
19					

Notes

Home:	Date:	Umpire:
Away:	Location:	Scorer:

#	Player	P	1	2	3	4	5	6	7	8	9	10	AB	H	BB	RBI	R
Runs																	

Lineup Card

Team	Opponent
Coach	Coach

Order	No.	Starter	Pos.	No.	Substitute
1					
2					
3					
4					
5					
6					
7					
8					
9					
10					
11					
12					
13					
14					
15					
16					
17					
18					
19					

Notes

Home:	Date:	Umpire:
Away:	Location:	Scorer:

#	Player	P	1	2	3	4	5	6	7	8	9	10	AB	H	BB	RBI	R
Runs																	

Lineup Card

Team	Opponent
Coach	Coach

Order	No.	Starter	Pos.	No.	Substitute
1					
2					
3					
4					
5					
6					
7					
8					
9					
10					
11					
12					
13					
14					
15					
16					
17					
18					
19					

Notes

Home:	Date:	Umpire:
Away:	Location:	Scorer:

#	Player	P	1	2	3	4	5	6	7	8	9	10	AB	H	BB	RBI	R
Runs																	

Lineup Card

Team	Opponent
Coach	Coach

Order	No.	Starter	Pos.	No.	Substitute
1					
2					
3					
4					
5					
6					
7					
8					
9					
10					
11					
12					
13					
14					
15					
16					
17					
18					
19					

Notes

Home:	Date:	Umpire:
Away:	Location:	Scorer:

#	Player	P	1	2	3	4	5	6	7	8	9	10	AB	H	BB	RBI	R
Runs																	

Lineup Card

Team	Opponent
Coach	Coach

Order	No.	Starter	Pos.	No.	Substitute
1					
2					
3					
4					
5					
6					
7					
8					
9					
10					
11					
12					
13					
14					
15					
16					
17					
18					
19					

Notes

Home:	Date:	Umpire:
Away:	Location:	Scorer:

#	Player	P	1	2	3	4	5	6	7	8	9	10	AB	H	BB	RBI	R
Runs																	

Lineup Card

Team	Opponent
Coach	Coach

Order	No.	Starter	Pos.	No.	Substitute
1					
2					
3					
4					
5					
6					
7					
8					
9					
10					
11					
12					
13					
14					
15					
16					
17					
18					
19					

Notes

Home:	Date:	Umpire:
Away:	Location:	Scorer:

#	Player	P	1	2	3	4	5	6	7	8	9	10	AB	H	BB	RBI	R
Runs																	

Lineup Card

Team	Opponent
Coach	Coach

Order	No.	Starter	Pos.	No.	Substitute
1					
2					
3					
4					
5					
6					
7					
8					
9					
10					
11					
12					
13					
14					
15					
16					
17					
18					
19					

Notes

Home:	Date:	Umpire:
Away:	Location:	Scorer:

#	Player	P	1	2	3	4	5	6	7	8	9	10	AB	H	BB	RBI	R
Runs																	

Lineup Card

Team	Opponent
Coach	Coach

Order	No.	Starter	Pos.	No.	Substitute
1					
2					
3					
4					
5					
6					
7					
8					
9					
10					
11					
12					
13					
14					
15					
16					
17					
18					
19					

Notes

Home:	Date:	Umpire:
Away:	Location:	Scorer:

#	Player	P	1	2	3	4	5	6	7	8	9	10	AB	H	BB	RBI	R
Runs																	

Lineup Card

Team	Opponent
Coach	Coach

Order	No.	Starter	Pos.	No.	Substitute
1					
2					
3					
4					
5					
6					
7					
8					
9					
10					
11					
12					
13					
14					
15					
16					
17					
18					
19					

Notes

Home:	Date:	Umpire:
Away:	Location:	Scorer:

#	Player	P	1	2	3	4	5	6	7	8	9	10	AB	H	BB	RBI	R
Runs																	

Lineup Card

Team	Opponent
Coach	Coach

Order	No.	Starter	Pos.	No.	Substitute
1					
2					
3					
4					
5					
6					
7					
8					
9					
10					
11					
12					
13					
14					
15					
16					
17					
18					
19					

Notes

Home:	Date:	Umpire:
Away:	Location:	Scorer:

#	Player	P	1	2	3	4	5	6	7	8	9	10	AB	H	BB	RBI	R
Runs																	

Lineup Card

Team	Opponent
Coach	Coach

Order	No.	Starter	Pos.	No.	Substitute
1					
2					
3					
4					
5					
6					
7					
8					
9					
10					
11					
12					
13					
14					
15					
16					
17					
18					
19					

Notes

Home:	Date:	Umpire:
Away:	Location:	Scorer:

#	Player	P	1	2	3	4	5	6	7	8	9	10	AB	H	BB	RBI	R
Runs																	

Lineup Card

Team	Opponent
Coach	Coach

Order	No.	Starter	Pos.	No.	Substitute
1					
2					
3					
4					
5					
6					
7					
8					
9					
10					
11					
12					
13					
14					
15					
16					
17					
18					
19					

Notes

Home:	Date:	Umpire:
Away:	Location:	Scorer:

#	Player	P	1	2	3	4	5	6	7	8	9	10	AB	H	BB	RBI	R
Runs																	

Lineup Card

Team	Opponent
Coach	Coach

Order	No.	Starter	Pos.	No.	Substitute
1					
2					
3					
4					
5					
6					
7					
8					
9					
10					
11					
12					
13					
14					
15					
16					
17					
18					
19					

Notes

Home:	Date:	Umpire:
Away:	Location:	Scorer:

#	Player	P	1	2	3	4	5	6	7	8	9	10	AB	H	BB	RBI	R
Runs																	

Lineup Card

Team	Opponent
Coach	Coach

Order	No.	Starter	Pos.	No.	Substitute
1					
2					
3					
4					
5					
6					
7					
8					
9					
10					
11					
12					
13					
14					
15					
16					
17					
18					
19					

Notes

Home:	Date:	Umpire:
Away:	Location:	Scorer:

#	Player	P	1	2	3	4	5	6	7	8	9	10	AB	H	BB	RBI	R
Runs																	

Lineup Card

Team	Opponent
Coach	Coach

Order	No.	Starter	Pos.	No.	Substitute
1					
2					
3					
4					
5					
6					
7					
8					
9					
10					
11					
12					
13					
14					
15					
16					
17					
18					
19					

Notes

Home:	Date:	Umpire:
Away:	Location:	Scorer:

#	Player	P	1	2	3	4	5	6	7	8	9	10	AB	H	BB	RBI	R
Runs																	

Lineup Card

Team	Opponent
Coach	Coach

Order	No.	Starter	Pos.	No.	Substitute
1					
2					
3					
4					
5					
6					
7					
8					
9					
10					
11					
12					
13					
14					
15					
16					
17					
18					
19					

Notes

Home:	Date:	Umpire:
Away:	Location:	Scorer:

#	Player	P	1	2	3	4	5	6	7	8	9	10	AB	H	BB	RBI	R
Runs																	

Lineup Card

Team	Opponent
Coach	Coach

Order	No.	Starter	Pos.	No.	Substitute
1					
2					
3					
4					
5					
6					
7					
8					
9					
10					
11					
12					
13					
14					
15					
16					
17					
18					
19					

Notes

Home:	Date:	Umpire:
Away:	Location:	Scorer:

#	Player	P	1	2	3	4	5	6	7	8	9	10	AB	H	BB	RBI	R
Runs																	

Lineup Card

Team	Opponent
Coach	**Coach**

Order	No.	Starter	Pos.	No.	Substitute
1					
2					
3					
4					
5					
6					
7					
8					
9					
10					
11					
12					
13					
14					
15					
16					
17					
18					
19					

Notes

Home:	Date:	Umpire:
Away:	Location:	Scorer:

#	Player	P	1	2	3	4	5	6	7	8	9	10	AB	H	BB	RBI	R
Runs																	

Lineup Card

Team	Opponent
Coach	Coach

Order	No.	Starter	Pos.	No.	Substitute
1					
2					
3					
4					
5					
6					
7					
8					
9					
10					
11					
12					
13					
14					
15					
16					
17					
18					
19					

Notes

Home:	Date:	Umpire:
Away:	Location:	Scorer:

#	Player	P	1	2	3	4	5	6	7	8	9	10	AB	H	BB	RBI	R
Runs																	

Lineup Card

Team	Opponent
Coach	Coach

Order	No.	Starter	Pos.	No.	Substitute
1					
2					
3					
4					
5					
6					
7					
8					
9					
10					
11					
12					
13					
14					
15					
16					
17					
18					
19					

Notes

Home:	Date:	Umpire:
Away:	Location:	Scorer:

#	Player	P	1	2	3	4	5	6	7	8	9	10	AB	H	BB	RBI	R
Runs																	

Made in United States
Orlando, FL
11 April 2023

32002228R00057